52 Weekly Devotionals
To Heal And Strengthen Your Christian Relationship

Morgan Avery

Marriage Miracle

52 Weekly Devotionals to Heal and Strengthen Your Christian Relationship

By Morgan Avery

© 2011 Christian Book Council
All Rights Reserved.

Address:

KRE Book Group
PO Box 121135
Nashville, TN 37212-1135

ISBN-978-1-60842-202-9

MarriageMiracleOnline.com

✂ TABLE OF CONTENTS ✃

Introduction 5
Week 1 - Exodux 3:11-12 7
Week 2 - Genesis 2:18 9
Week 3 - Genesis 2:19-20 11
Week 4 - Genesis 2:23-24 13
Week 5 - Genesis 1:27 15
Week 6 - 1 Corinthians 13:1 17
Week 7 - 1 Corinthians 13 19
Week 8 - 1 Corinthians 13 21
Week 9 - 1 Corinthians 13 23
Week 10 - 1 Corinthians 13 25
Week 11 - 1 Corinthians 13 27
Week 12 - 1 Corinthians 13 29
Week 13 - 1 Corinthians 13 31
Week 14 - 1 Corinthians 13 33
Week 15 - 1 Corinthians 13 35
Week 16 - 1 Corinthians 13 37
Week 17 - 1 Corinthians 13 39
Week 18 - 1 Corinthians 13 41
Week 19 - 1 Corinthians 13 43
Week 20 - 1 Corinthians 13 45
Week 21 - 1 Corinthians 13 47
Week 22 - 1 Corinthians 13 49
Week 23 - 1 Corinthians 13 51
Week 24 - 1 Corinthians 13 53
Week 25 - Song of Solomon 4:9 55
Week 26 - Song of Solomon 4 57
Week 27 - Matthew 6 59
Week 28 - Matthew 6 61

TABLE OF CONTENTS - Cont'd

Week 29 - Matthew 6 63
Week 30 - Matthew 6 65
Week 31 - Song of Solomon 2 67
Week 32 - Song of Solomon 2 69
Week 33 - Song of Solomon 2 71
Week 34 - Song of Solomon 2 73
Week 35 - Song of Solomon 2 75
Week 36 - Song of Solomon 2 77
Week 37 - Song of Solomon 2 79
Week 38 - Romans 8:38-39 81
Week 39 - John 16 83
Week 40 - 1 Corinthians 12:14-20 85
Week 41 - 1 Corinthians 12:21 87
Week 42 - 1 Corinthians 12:26 89
Week 43 - Proverbs 14:1 91
Week 44 - Proverbs 15:1 93
Week 45 - Proverbs 15:4 95
Week 46 - James 4:8 97
Week 47 - 1 Peter 4:8 99
Week 48 - 1 Thessalonians 5:18 101
Week 49 - 1 John 4 103
Week 50 - 1 John 4 105
Week 51 - 1 John 4 107
Week 52 - Mark 12:30-31 109

INTRODUCTION

The journey of marriage takes us to both sublime and stubborn places. Even the best and brightest relationship has tough times. The most difficult marriages can have moments of warmth and beauty. It is a road that leads us beyond our expectations.

As Christians, we have the assurance that God is walking with us on that grand highway. If only we will lift our eyes from the pavement and look for him! There is so much help and encouragement available but we so often try to go it alone. My hope (and purpose) in writing these weekly devotions is that you will feel the encouragement that is present in scripture, and through the power of the Holy Spirit you will feel refreshed. Accepted and refreshed.

We are often worried that our lives are not perfect. Well, they aren't. There you have it. Let it go. The choice is not whether to be perfect or terrible. Our choice is to make the best decisions we can and to keep putting one foot in front of the other.

Accepting that marriage is not a state of being, but rather a river that is constantly winding and turning and twisting with surprises, releasing us from having to stand in a posture that is not true. Devotion to marriage means getting your paddle out and using it. Devotion to marriage means if you fall out of the canoe, crawl back in. Devotion to marriage means enjoy the view.

As a companion piece to the book "Christian Relationships," this devotional guide is designed to encourage the ongoing devotion to marriage. Some of the entries are quite serious and challenging, others are light and written to remind you to lighten up. Use them as you will. They are meant to be your friends.

If you can read these devotions with your spouse, great. If not, don't worry. There is no "method" to reach marital bliss. Read and enjoy.

1

"**But Moses said to God, 'Who am I, that I should go to Pharaoh and bring the Israelites out of Egypt?'**

And God said, 'I will be with you.'"

(Exodus 3:11-12)

The bottom line is this: If you are on a spiritual journey you will have company. The company of God is constant and yet ever changing. In my experience God seems to appear in the form of feeling, strangers, loved ones, music, random events, dreams, thoughts and a thousand other manifestations. But as long as I stay on the path of love and compassion that Jesus calls me on, I have company.

Imagine God asking you to go to the land of Egypt and lead the Israelites out of slavery into a new land and a new future. A daunting task; similar to marriage. "Who am I," Moses mutters rolling his eyes and backing away, "to do such a thing?" You might say the same thing about your marriage. Who are you to bring your marriage back from the brink of despair? Who are you to sustain a marriage decade after decade? Who are you to live a real marriage that defies all predictions of boredom, gloom and doom?

The answer is a simple one, though not an easy one! God doesn't answer, "I will do it for you!" Wouldn't that be nice! No. God says, "I will be with you."

That means that God believes you can do it. And will be walking by your side every step of the way.

So it is this lightening strike of confidence that we begin the devotional study on Christian marriage and relationship. How can we do this?

God is with us.

PRAYER:

Dear God, What can I say but I am surprised and I am thankful. In my struggle, in my real life, you are here. You are not afraid of the challenge. You have not given up on me. I bring myself, my marriage, and my whole life to you. I will go, if you lead me. I pray this in the name of Jesus, Amen.

2

> "*And* the Lord God said, 'It is not good that man should be alone; I will make a helpmate for him...'"
>
> (Genesis 2:18)

Modern women often shudder at this verse. Helpmate? Hmmph! The whole sequence of events seems to put women in a subordinate and second-class position. Actually, there is no denying that. In the creation story it seems that God thought of men first and women second. I don't know why. It's one of the questions I'd like to ask when I get face to face.

I want to point out that the word *helpmate* is a word used later in the Bible to refer to God. God is the helpmate of Israel. So, if God can be a helpmate, hey, it must not be too subordinate!

But that may not be enough for many modern women. It's a tough question and I'm not going to pretend otherwise. However, I can stay stuck in that question or I can look at the text for the doors that do open for me. Look at this verse again. Focus on this, "It is not good that man should be alone." Now the door opens.

It is not good that man should be alone. The full, rich life includes other people. And a marriage is about as "unalone" as one can get! If God is love and we want to know God then we need to be in circumstances where love can flow. Sure, it can flow when we are alone. But in this creation scripture God points out that it is not good to be alone. These creatures, God seems to say, need companionship. They need mates. They need intimacy. And help!

If I want to know God I don't have to go outside and look up at the stars and wonder. I can roll over and look at my sleeping spouse. And in the love that lives in me, as I watch him, I can experience the breath of God, the promise, and the presence.

How close it all is – the presence of God. If we pay attention.

PRAYER:

God, help me pay attention. You have created this world so that we might have life and have it in abundance, so that we might have love and have it all around us. Help me see and feel that. Help me reach past my aloneness and connect to my husband/wife as you planned when time began. In the name of Jesus, Amen.

3

> "And the Lord God caused a deep sleep to fall upon Adam, and he slept: and he took one of his ribs, and closed up the flesh instead thereof; and the rib, which the Lord God had taken from man, made a woman, and brought her unto the man."
>
> (Genesis 2:19-20)

Men and women are made from the same substance. As different as we are, and we certainly seem like completely different species sometimes, we are essentially the same creature.

When my son was born and was a mere month old, my husband took him out for a walk late one night. At the time, we were staying with a wonderful couple, farm people, who had raised a big family and now had many grandchildren. I was sitting in the living room with the wife when my husband came back in with my son.

"We went for a walk across the frozen pond!" my husband said with enthusiasm.

My heart stopped. *He took my child across a frozen pond in the middle of the night?* I was horrified beyond belief. I expressed my horror and reached out for my child. My husband slunk off to bed feeling rather bad about what he had done.

I sat in the living room, holding my son and feeling very angry.

"That's what men do," she said to me in her soft, warm voice.

I looked up and the wife of this couple was smiling across the room at me.

"They push the limits. If we could, we would keep our children in our arms their whole lives!" she said laughing.

She continued and helped me see that men and women have different things to give to children. Women protect. Men push and encourage.

How many times have I gone back to that as a parent as I watched the different way a father raises a child! We are of the same substance – we both love our children and yet we have different points of view. Different ways.

Of one substance yet formed by God to be distinctly different.

In marriage, we are to be distinctly different.

PRAYER:

Dear God, Give me the wisdom to embrace our differences. We may be formed of the same substance, and yet you have given us separate points of view – d.ifferences that are necessary. Let me give my husband/wife the freedom to be what she/he is created to be. In Jesus name, Amen.

4

"nd Adam said, 'This is now bone of my bones, and flesh of my flesh: she shall be called Woman, because she was taken out of Man. Therefore shall a man leave his father and his mother and shall cleave unto his wife.'"

(Genesis 2:23-24)

***Cleave*: To cling closely, steadfastly, faithfully.**

Nice word. Young couples do it so well. Sitting behind a young couple in the park the other day I watched as they clung to one another. There was never a moment when some part of their bodies wasn't touching. They were so aware of each other. When she got up, he was her shadow. He wrapped his arms around her and they walked off as if in a three-legged race.

Why do we stop touching each other after a few years of marriage? Why do we stop telling each other, "I love you" 10 times a day? Why do we begin to take it all for granted?

That young couple was lost in the wonder that someone so wonderful might love them. That truth is still with those of us in middle age but we so often forget to be grateful for it.

I sat in a nursing home the other day with a 90-year-old woman. Her ancient hands were stretched out on her lap. She had a simple gold ring on each hand. One was her wedding ring, of course, but I asked what the other one was.

"It's his wedding ring," she answered. She stretched her hands out in front of her and then looked up at me with shining eyes. "He was a wonderful man!" she said.

How she would have touched him, if he had been there. How she would have cleaved to him. She was cleaving, clinging, faithfully and steadfastly, even now.

PRAYER:

Dear God, Give me the awareness to be grateful for my marriage every day. Let me not fall into the great abyss of forgetfulness and fuss. In Jesus name, Amen.

5

"So God created man in his own image, in the image of God he created him; male and female he created them."

(Genesis 1:27)

What is the image of God? A creative power that imagined and breathed into existence all that is, that was and that shall be! And we are created in this image? Evidently. We are created in the image of the one who comes up with the duckbilled platypus, the vast array of the universe, the humming of a toddler, the power of the sun, the delicate balance of color in a budding rose, and all other marvels that you and I have ever seen.

What f we brought creativity, God's kind of creativity, to our marriages? What if we refused to stop at "what was" and started making up new stuff? What if we worked our way through and around the mess and static problems around us with a gleeful childlike spirit?

In marriage we get into so many ruts. Rituals and routines are useful in creating a peaceful domestic life but there also must be room for surprise! Sexual intimacy in marriage is a place where creativity should constantly bloom. And yet so often we lapse into old patterns and stop playing.

Sexual intimacy can be a time when a couple sheds all the responsibilities and routines that adult life imposes upon us and simply plays. Like children. Without shame. With lots of laughter. Lots of passion. Lots of imagination.

Here in the safe arms of our marriage we re-create the Garden of Eden. We are Adam and Eve, playing in the garden, full of laughter and silly ideas. We are simply human, fully passionate, trusting in each other's arms, just as God created us to be – in his wildly imaginative image. We are running full and fast, loving hard and soft, laughing, crying, nothing held back. And when we find this space with our mate – this place of bliss and ancient home – we are for a moment – God's image.

PRAYER:

Dear God, May I find the Garden of Eden again – in my life – in the arms of my spouse. Give me the courage to be creative, to be a child, to be free again and to be in your image. In Jesus name, Amen.

6

"*If* I speak in the tongues of mortals and of angels, but do not have love, I am a noisy gong or a clanging cymbal."

(1 Corinthians 13:1)

Talk is cheap. Communication is golden. There is a lot of empty talk in marriage. We throw phrases around with ease. The usual, "Love ya!" at the end of a phone conversation or little endearing terms like "Honey" and "Sweetheart." Often a marriage will build up a façade that looks very happy and yet t is paper-thin because there is no authentic meaning behind the words.

In this scripture the Apostle Paul is referring to speaking beautifully, sounding good, having all the "right" words and yet, without love filling up the sound, the surface is paper-thin. Just noise.

Sometimes I listen to a couple talking "love" but I see a different story in their lives, in their body language, in the choices they make, and in the atmosphere they create around them. I catch myself doing it – saying something sweet to cover up the truth underneath.

It can work for a while. Ultimately, however, the truth will come out. A marriage that is not healthy is not ultimately sustainable. The health of each person will suffer. Other parts of life will begin to unravel. All the effort that it's taking to smooth over the surface is being borrowed from another part of one's life. If there are children, they will begin to show the signs of neglect because something is wrong at the heart of their parents' marriage.

> **The truth will set you free.**

Love tells the truth. It's not easy to tell the truth – but in the long run it is the best choice. Making oneself vulnerable to the person who shares our life can be tough. Smoothing the surface seems like a better answer in the moment, but over time it is exhausting. It's like telling a lie – it takes constant effort to remember and lies build and the complexity of keeping the surface smooth becomes overwhelming.

If you speak the truth, with love, in your marriage, there will be beautiful music. And it will sing on its own – you won't have to tend to it daily – covering up that which is difficult. Trust the truth. The truth will set you free.

PRAYER:

Dear God, I ask for the courage to speak the truth in love. Help me to trust that love is enough and resist the temptation to make everything look angelic and perfect. Help me to trust that love is the answer. In Jesus name, Amen.

7

"And if I have prophetic powers, and understand all mysteries and all knowledge, and if I have all faith, so as to remove mountains, but do not have love, I am nothing."

(1 Corinthians 13)

Let me tell you a secret – ministers have a really tough time in marriage. So do marriage counselors. So do people who write books about it, and those who research and study marriage. You can know everything about a subject, you can talk pretty and understand what is wrong with everyone's marriage and you can be a fountain of wisdom and advice – but still – you can have a really rough time in marriage.

Knowledge is not love. Even having tons of faith, as the scripture puts it, so much faith so as to remove mountains, does not equal having love. Remember the kind of love that the Apostle Paul is talking about here is Agape love. The love that is God centered –

that is unconditional love. Agape does not depend upon external events. It is the love that flows through us when we open our hearts and stop relying upon our own powers of knowledge, faith and human strength.

One of the reasons we follow the Christian path is we know our own resources are not enough. To truly live, to live fully and to experience what this life is really about, we need a connection with God. We need the love that we find in spiritual connection with God far beyond our own individual power to generate.

The minister, counselor and writer can stand by the river and discuss it. They can predict what the river will do when the rains come, and they understand the river to a certain extent. They know what it is made of. They know it has power. But unless they actually fall into the river and are swept away by the current, they know nothing.

Fall into the current that is God. Fall into the powerful stream of unconditional love that is God. Be swept away. Be lost in love for your husband or wife that is far beyond anything you know or can understand.

Don't be a bystander in your own marriage. Don't stand on the riverbank and criticize and analyze and predict and converse. Jump in. Be in love.

PRAYER:

Dear God, I want to be in the love that is you. I want to be in love in my marriage. Push me in the river, God! Throw me in! I surrender to your love and leave all my little human knowing on the shoreline. In Jesus name, Amen.

8

"*If* I give away all my possessions, and if I hand over my body so that I may boast, but do not have love, I gain nothing."

(1 Corinthians 13)

Oh, the martyrs I have seen stoically putting up with a difficult husband or wife. Oh the sacrifice they show on their faces!

"Oh what I have to deal with!" they whisper behind the back of their spouse.

A woman came to me recently and said, "I have given up my whole life for this man and he doesn't even notice. I've given up the things I like to do. I've given up who I am, practically! What more can I do?"

I wanted to say, "Doesn't sound like there is much left to love! You gave yourself away? What's to notice?" I didn't say that because it wouldn't have helped her but I'm sure I raised an eyebrow.

Loving someone doesn't mean sacrificing everything that you hold dear. Remember, Jesus already did the big sacrifice for us – we don't need to climb up on a cross every day. He did that so that we might have life. Our job is to have life. And have it in abundance, if you remember!

Sacrifice is part of marriage. An older woman had a stroke that left her unable to walk or speak and so her husband made the difficult decision to have her live at the nursing home where she could have round the clock care. He came every morning, drove down an hour, and was there when she woke up. He dressed her. Fed her breakfast. Spent the day with her. He read the newspaper to her. Got her in the wheelchair and went for long walks. He sat with her in the evening and talked about their life, about people they knew. They called their children every night on the phone and she would listen. He dressed her for bed and tucked her in and then drove home. He did this for three years until the day she died.

Was that sacrifice? Yes. Was it martyrdom? No. He loved being with her. It took effort, absolutely, but it was fueled by his actual love and affection for her.

There is nothing to gain from suffering as a martyr except bitterness. Do not give yourself away. Do not stop doing the things you love. Do not give yourself up for another person. You will not gain anything. You will lose your life. Get off the cross. Go do something that makes you happy.

PRAYER:

Dear God, You have given me my life. It is a gift. Help me to enjoy it and not waste it in anger and bitterness. You died on the cross so that I might have life. Give me the courage to live my own life. In Jesus name, Amen.

 is patient."

(1 Corinthians 13)

He sits in the car outside the church. It's a cold day and he has the engine on. I stop and he rolls down the window.

"Waiting for your wife?" I say.

"Yup," he answers with a smile.

We talk for a while. She doesn't come out. We talk longer.

"Do you want me to go in and find her?" I finally say.

"Oh no. She'll come out eventually. It's all right," he laughs.

"She does this a lot?" I ask.

"Oh yes. Always has," he says.

"How long have you been married?" I inquire.

"Fifty-two years," he says evenly.

"And she's always keeping you waiting?" I say.

"That's who she is," he answers.

"And you don't get mad about it?" I ask.

"What good would that do? I'm okay. I find things to do. I'm talking to you aren't I?" he laughs hard.

We talk on for quite a while. Finally she comes out of the church and he gets out of the car and goes around to help her put stuff in the trunk and then gets her in the front seat. On his way back to the driver's seat he winks at me and says, "See! I knew she'd come out eventually!"

As they drive off I marvel at his patience. He simply accepts her for who she is. Maybe he tried early on in their marriage to get her to hurry up or maybe he never did. I don't know. What I know is that he was not upset about it. He was at peace. He didn't take it personally. He simply saw that this was her way. It wasn't a slight or insult to him. He let her be who she is. And he found a way to pass the time that pleased him.

Love is patient. To love someone as they are is an art form. Day by day we can take away our bitterness and our anger by not taking things personally. Our husband or wife is not on earth to make us crazy. They are simply being who they are. And we must be who we are. And let the love that is patient flow through us.

PRAYER:

Dear God, Help me to release all bitterness and anger and let your love flow through me. There is no hurry. I ask your help to be in the moment, in the day, and not always rushing ahead of myself. Bless me, O Lord, with the love that is patient. In Jesus name, Amen.

(1 Corinthians 13)

One of the things that Paul is doing in Corinthians 13 is teaching us how to recognize agape love. There was a pop song in the 1970s titled, "How will I know?" The lyrics were "How will I know if he really loves me? I'm asking you cause you know about these things. How will I know if he really cares?"

Paul says that there are ways to recognize agape love. First – it is kind. What kind of tree is it? Look at what fruit it bears. Does it bear fruit that is kind? Look at the people and activities surrounding a marriage or a person. Are they emotionally healthy? Have they been treated with kindness? Are they trusting?

A dysfunctional family or marriage is often rotating around something very far from kindness. The primary energy between two people or between family members is revealed in the resulting lives of those who are involved.

There are many other "realities" that disguise themselves as love. Possessive or controlling behavior often masks itself as true love, passionate love, and it can appear at first glance to be agape love. Paul would suggest that you look at the lives of the persons who are touched by this "reality." A person who has been loved with agape love, which is essentially kind, is calm. A child who has been loved with agape love is confident. There is no need for self-soothing behavior like drugs and alcohol because at heart there is no fear and there is no pain.

Other "realities" cause pain. They are not kind because those types of energies are selfish and uninterested in the needs of the persons they are directed at. Kindness comes from a selfless type of love. The person who lets agape love flow through them does not need his/her loved ones to act in a particular way. Agape love is kind because it is unconnected to the behavior of the one receiving it. It is like a mighty river that does not dry up when expectations are not met. It is always there.

At a funeral last weekend for the quiet, much respected patriarch of a large family, the words I heard most were this: "He was always there." This is a sign of agape love. The family felt his kindness because his presence was always there no matter what choices they made. He was kind. He was there. He loved them no matter what the weather, no matter what the time of day, no matter what the crisis or victory. And the fruits of his ability to love in this way sat there in the church – pew after pew of healthy, loving families, a marriage of 70 years, and a church full of respect, grief and honor.

PRAYER:

Dear God, Love through me. I open up my heart and soul and ask that your powerful love, which is unending and not dependent upon the actions of others, might roll through the choices of my day. I seek to be kind. In Jesus name, Amen.

11

"*Love* is not envious."

(1 Corinthians 13)

Life is not fair. Some of us are more visibly and publicly rewarded than others. In marriage this can be a tough area. We are proud of our spouse and yet ...

"He gets all the attention," she said looking over at her husband who was surrounded by a group of admirers. "I'm proud of him, of course, but if they only knew how much I had to do with it all!"

I was speaking with the wife of a prominent minister. She was dressed modestly, and sitting in the back row of the church. He was up front, having just come down after a service in which he preached a spectacular sermon.

"Did you help him with that sermon?" I asked as I sat next to her.

"Yes. Yes I did – and a thousand other things. I know I shouldn't feel this way. I certainly shouldn't say anything but sometimes ..." she stopped and sat in silence as she looked down at her hands.

In this situation – no one was doing anything wrong. Her husband was not abusing her by shining in public. She wanted to help him! They were a great team. She was simply feeling envious. It is a natural human emotion.

But it isn't love. She was struggling with her ego.

The ego is an important part of human survival. It alerts us to dangers. In the past it would alert us to lions rustling in the grass. Now that life is not quite so clear cut it alerts us to anything it sees as dangerous. Emotional threats and life's unfairness are seen with the same clarity as the outline of a lion against the moon.

The ego is not where agape love flows from, however. It is a handy warning light, yes, and doesn't need to be disregarded entirely. However, when we are looking for love, if we are feeling envy – beware. That is the ego talking.

We sat in silence in the back row of the church, watching her husband shake hands and have conversations with people. I felt what she was feeling.

Then her husband glanced over the heads of the group that was standing around him and he saw her. He excused himself and walked down the aisle. He reached us and he held out his arms to her. She stood and went to him. He wrapped his arms around her and looked down and said, "How did we do?"

"We did great!" she said smiling. Her face was suddenly filled with light and he pulled her in close and held her tight.

And so envy was vanquished, the lion scared off, and agape love was victorious.

PRAYER:

Dear God, I know there will be times that I am envious of my spouse. Help me to live through it and get to a better place quickly. Help me to see that envy is as thin as paper, and love as thick as the whole spinning earth. In Jesus name, Amen.

12

(1 Corinthians 13)

She listens to him every night when he comes home. They sit at the table and he tells her of his day. The children listen. They all listen as he rattles off the details of how well he did and how smoothly everything went.

She knows, of course, that what he is saying isn't true. He has a difficult job, not one that he wants, and things often don't go well. He is struggling simply to stay employed. He is very frightened that he is going to be let go at any time.

As he talks, she watches him closely. His hands are shaky as he cuts his meat. His face is red. He talks loudly and laughs often at things that aren't actually funny. After supper he goes immediately to the television and gets lost in it for the rest of the evening. She knows he doesn't want to feel anything because he feels so badly.

He comes to bed. They lie there quietly, looking out the window at the full moon.

"Hi," she finally says.

"Hi," he says.

And then he turns to her and crawls into her arms and she holds him so tight.

"What are we doing to do?" he whispers. "What am I going to do?"

She kisses him and says, "We're in this together. We're going to make it."

That's love. When boasts fail and truth emerges. When trust is deep enough that secrets and fears are seen for what they are. Past the posturing and the boasting, past the fears and the anxieties, past the performance – there is a place where a marriage can be alive.

In that place, in the beauty of intimacy, we can let go of what we thought we would be. We can stop trying to live up to the expectations of others and we can be ourselves.

The gift of God to humans is that in the middle of this world, where things are fragile and the way is not always clear, we have company. And in the company, if we will work to be truthful, to let go of boasting and all pride, we can experience what God is – unconditional, life-sustaining, soul-strengthening love.

PRAYER:

Dear God, Grant me the strength to be vulnerable with my husband/wife. I know there are times when I have to dance the dance in this world, and pretend that I know what I am doing. But give me the strength to release all that at the heart of my marriage and in doing so – find you. In Jesus name, Amen.

13

"*Love* is not arrogant."

(1 Corinthians 13)

Arrogance. An overlooked point in Corinthians 13. And yet, in fact, it may be at the heart of what Paul is trying to convey. Arrogance is the solid belief that I am able. I am able to understand, to comprehend, to do, and to be that which I want to be. I. I. I. It is the absolute belief that the solid ground I stand on comes from my own smarty-pants goodness.

Humph.

In reality, love, agape true unconditional love, does not come from our own intelligence, genetic predisposition or even a great upbringing. Agape love comes from God. That's all there is to it. So this phrase, "Love is not arrogant" might be translated into, "Love is not my own invention."

Love comes through us – if we let it. Our choice is not whether we can manufacture good love – good enough love – better love – best love! No. Our choice is whether we can let the love of God flow through us.

To let love flow through us means two things:

1. We must be connected to God. We must reach for the source of agape love.
2. We must be humble.

To be humble means that we don't need to share every thought that comes into our heads. We don't need to act on every feeling. We can make choices. Loving choices. The mature Christian strives for the ability to discern when an action is coming from our lower nature (survival instinct, ego) or our higher nature (that which is connected to God).

A practicing Christian (marvelous image – practicing in order to become better at it!) sees each day, each event as a chance to refine his/her skills at discernment. In marriage we are offered many opportunities each day to choose how to respond or how to act toward our spouse. It is a wonderful training ground! (Especially if forgiveness abounds!)

Arrogance would have us believe that we are the source of love. If we can let go of our own arrogance, our own belief that we somehow are responsible for generating agape love, then we can allow the love that comes from God to flow through us and to fill our lives, our spouses and our families with light.

PRAYER:

Dear God, Not my will, but thy will be done. Help me to see when I am stuck in my own small needs. Give me the courage to brush away feelings and thoughts that are centered in my own arrogance. In Jesus name, Amen.

(1 Corinthians 13)

We are at coffee hour after the church service. I am standing with a couple that has recently joined the congregation.

"So, will you be taking a vacation this year?" I ask.

"With him? No way. I need a vacation from him," the wife answers stridently.

He laughs and looks away.

"Oh," I am not sure how to proceed. "Well ... how are you feeling here at church? Are you finding yourself at home?"

"I guess so but I wish he'd stay home!" she rolls her eyes and they both laugh. "Just look at him! I don't want to be seen with that!"

She waves her hand at her husband's body, gesturing up and down, and then simply pointing at his stomach. "Look at him, he doesn't even take care of himself!"

They both laugh.

I felt sick, actually, watching his face. What she said, and the way she said it, was so deeply humiliating. And for it to come from someone who knows him so well! From someone who should, as we say, have his back. I didn't know what to do. It was such blatant rudeness. In my mind, as I stood there, I simply prayed for them. I have no idea what the deeper story was, but obviously there was one.

But they taught me a very powerful lesson.

When we are married to someone we are given great power to either wound or heal. It is our choice. And because we are "standing so close" we have the ability to deeply hurt or to deeply heal.

Rude comments, denigrating even in laughter, come from a deep anger and never from love. If you find yourself saying things, even if it is in the guise of "letting off steam" it is time to turn and contemplate the source that generated these thoughts and feelings.

We all fall into this trap – from time to time – and the first thing is to immediately ask forgiveness from our spouse and anyone else who heard us. Second, face the feelings and situations that gave rise to such rudeness. For something to slip out in conversation means it has a reality in your life. Use the mistake to find your way – like a compass – back to the source of the anger. Our mistakes often will lead us directly to the problem.

PRAYER:

Dear God, Forgive me for the times I have been rude. I ask for guidance, to follow the signpost of my errors and trace the way back to the source of the problem. Give me the courage to face the deeper issues in my marriage and in my life. In Jesus name, Amen.

15

> *"It does not insist upon its own way."*
>
> (1 Corinthians 13)

"She's got the inside and I've got the outside," the farmer told me. We were standing by the barn, a ramshackle but sturdy structure. His face was deeply lined, tanned brown by the sun and whipped red by the wind. He looked up at me and he grinned. "I don't mess with her and she don't mess with me."

We went together into to the kitchen. He stopped in the breezeway to take off his shoes and jacket. The kitchen was warm. There was a wood stove blazing. She was standing behind the counter putting together some sandwiches for us

"Sit down now, Pastor," she sang out as she slapped mayonnaise and ham on the bread. He took his place, I took mine and she served us.

"I was asking your husband about why he thinks your marriage has worked so well all these years," I said when she sat down.

"Oh. He says it works well? Glad to hear that," she laughed.

"Yes. He says it's because he's got the outside and you've got the inside. Both of you have areas where you make decisions and where you decide things."

"Yes. I think that's true. We know who is good at what," she answered.

It may seem simplistic but traditional marriage has always had segregation in terms of who is in power where. A good marriage shares power. We all need power. We all need to shine at what we're good at. Traditional marriage made those categories so clear that there was no questioning it. Modern marriage has begun to question it.

It's a good thing to question socially imposed structures! My generation has reinvented marriage. The old areas – men outside/women inside – have fallen by the wayside. Everybody gets his or her own way every place. And it has been, in many ways, a mess. Does this mean we need to return to the old ways? No. There are women who are actually better working outside the home. They are happier and using their God-given gifts. And there are men who are wonderfully nurturing and excellent at domestic bliss. We have won the freedom to cross over those old boundaries.

But the concept of boundary, respecting each other's ability to be in charge of various areas of life, this is something that we shouldn't lose. When we lose boundaries we lose the respect that traditional marriage has instilled in it for both persons. Teamwork thrives on each person using his/her God-given gifts. The loss of boundary, however, creates situations in which one person can become dominant and want "their own way" in everything.

PRAYER:

Dear God, Help me find boundaries in my marriage. I don't need to have my own way everyplace. Help me let go of the things that are not mine to watch over. Help me respect my spouse. Teach me to love in this way. In Jesus name, Amen.

16

"*It* does not insist upon its own way." (Take Two!)

(1 Corinthians 13)

When she got married, Marianne brought with her a hundred romantic ideas about what her marriage would be. She brought the image of her own parents and how they related to each other. She brought all the sentimental movies that she had watched as a young woman. She brought a belief that once she was married everything would be happy and easy.

What do you think happened?

She became disillusioned. Who was this man? Where did the attentive, exciting suitor go? What happened to the man she married? This man was so ordinary, full of burping and often very grouchy. Worst of all, he suddenly had all these crazy ideas about whom she should be and what she was supposed to do.

Naturally she was devastated. When she came in for counseling she was ready to leave. I noted that her husband hadn't come with her. She answered that she didn't tell him she was coming to talk with me.

"Why not?" I inquired.

"I don't know. It's not really his business, is it? The whole thing is a mess," she said hopelessly.

"Have you tried talking with him about things?" I asked. "About how things are going in your marriage?"

"No! There's no use. He's not who I thought he was. I don't want to be married anymore!" she answered as her eyes filled with tears.

I looked at her, a young woman so full of hope and dreams, wanting to have a good life. She was not a bad person! She was simply facing that moment that we all face: This isn't how I thought it was going to be.

In fact, that is one of the basic truths of life: it isn't how we thought it was going to be.

It's important to pay attention to our grief at the way things are. We get ourselves into unhealthy situations. Changes need to be made. But more often, we are simply scared because we thought we knew what we were getting into.

We'll continue to follow Marianne in the next few devotions. For now, I would simply say that disillusionment is part of an important spiritual process. It is the letting go of "How I thought it was going to be."

PRAYER:

Dear God, I had this plan and it doesn't seem to be working out. Help me to trust you and to let go of my little vision for my life. Help me to see my life clearly, without the filter of my expectations. In Jesus name, Amen.

17

"*Love* is not irritable or resentful."

(1 Corinthians 13)

Marianne began a process of peeling back her expectations. It took a lot of honest work on her part and she was very brave in looking at what she thought marriage was going to be and whom she thought her husband was.

The stage of disillusionment is very important because it helps us let go of our own plan. We then can start to enter God's reality – the plan that is given to us. If we stay in our own plan we will absolutely live a life that is tinged or filled with irritability and resentment. Our own plan is almost always doomed to be disappointing.

However, if we can release our grasp from the small vision of our own minds and hearts, then we might be able to look up and see what is actually in our life – and who is actually there.

No husband deserves to be a figment of your imagination. Who can live up to the romantic aspirations of a young wife? Men need to be loved as they are – burps, fears, bumblings and brilliance. To love in an unconditional way means that we are not always comparing our spouse to who they might be or who we imagined them to be when we were dating.

No wife deserves to be a fantasy. Women can't live up to a constant expectation of perfection – physical, emotional or sexual! Wives also need to be loved as they are – in all their complexity and worries!

Marianne entered a time of depression. I encouraged her to find support among her women friends, to spend time in prayer every day and to stay in counseling. She did. It was tough. She had to grieve the plans she had made for her life. But she came out on the other side a much more mature person – a person who was ready to love what is, to love the man who was standing opposite her – the real man.

The resentment and bitterness that had filled her when she first started coming in gradually left. There was an emptiness. A void. It was not easy for her to step away from the blueprint she had carefully drawn for her life. I was very proud of her as she began to become more vulnerable. God became real to her in a way she had never expected.

"It's like we're in this together, me and God. I feel the presence of God because I need Him. I am looking for Him and I am finding Him," she said one day.

Her relationship with her husband changed dramatically. She began to tell him the truth of what she was feeling. It turned out he was feeling many of the same things. They found a friendship that started to grow and their marriage began to be real. Her resentment changed into surprise and often delight at the very real, and actually quite wonderful man she was married to!

PRAYER:

Dear God, Lead me. I'm letting go of my plan. It's scary. Where are you? Help me to find and trust you. In Jesus name, Amen.

18

"It does not rejoice in wrongdoing."
(1 Corinthians 13)

Marianne and her husband were now on a path of honesty and clarity. Was everything fixed and easy?

No. There were struggles. There was a very, very big struggle.

Her husband lost his job because he had been found to be embezzling small amounts of cash each week. He was very repentant and paid the money back immediately and so his company did not press charges. Nonetheless, in our small community, word got around. Not only was he unemployed, but it was going to be very hard for him to find work again.

Marianne's family was very worried and began to encourage her to leave the marriage. There were no children yet, and they had been married only a few years. They knew that she had been struggling with the marriage and they felt that her worries were confirmed with this situation. Marianne was, quite honestly, furious.

"I knew there was something wrong with him! I knew it!" she said in an almost victorious tone. "I should have left before all this happened."

She was angry. She was angry with me for encouraging her to work on her marriage. She was angry with her husband. She was also angry with God.

"Is this God's big plan?" she snapped one day, "Is this his grand design?"

I wanted to say, "Probably!" but I thought she might throw something at me. So I shrugged my shoulders. What I noticed, however, as I observed her in those early weeks, was a kind of rejoicing – a dark kind of rejoicing. There was part of her – the controlling, angry part – that was pleased to be vindicated.

There is a saying, "You can be right or you can be happy." I sensed that she suddenly felt "right." And she was expanding that rather dark rejoicing into self-righteousness.

Being righteous means meaning in right relation to God. It does not mean being right. In the realm of love, the terms "right" and "wrong" are not quite so harshly defined as in the world of human justice. Jesus was constantly challenging the starkly black/white justice of the law by crossing over the lines and choosing to love unconditionally. But we have a hard time following him.

There is something satisfying in being right – in seeing the weaknesses of others and almost rejoicing in our superiority over them. In marriage this is surely one of the most destructive tendencies.

My deep sense was that God's plan included Marianne's facing this difficult situation. Here she had a chance to practice unconditional love. Would she?

PRAYER:

Dear God, Some things have happened that are really tough. I don't understand why. Why me? Help me surrender and listen. Give me the patience to learn how to love. Help me. In Jesus name, Amen.

19

"It rejoices in the truth."

(1 Corinthians 13)

Marianne moved out of her home went back to her parent's house.

"I can't think clearly," she said, "when he's there in front of me I just can't see straight. I'm so mad."

I encouraged her to take her time. Not to make any decisions right away but to let the dust settle. I also offered her the chance to be part of a small support group at church. I spoke to some of the "great hearts" in our church and they agreed to meet with Marianne and her husband, to pray, to support and to seek God's will.

As Christians we are as prone as anyone to shame and we will so easily retreat from facing our problems. We run. But we don't have to. Jesus showed us how important community is. Breaking bread with others who are on a similar journey is one of the most powerful ways to heal and to find God's path. We have to be careful and choose mature Christians in whom to confide our deepest struggles, but God always provides community and support if only we will accept it.

It was hard for Marianne and her husband to come to the first small group meeting. They came in with cast-down eyes and they were both very quiet. At one point her husband simply covered his face with his hands and wept.

Not much was said at that first group. There was a lot of silence and simply being together. But what they found was a place where they could speak the truth. After a few meetings Marianne's husband began to open up and tell his story. It was a hard story to tell and very hard to hear. His life had not been easy. He had been hiding a very difficult childhood and he was in a great deal of pain and confusion.

The group simply listened to him. They did not judge. In face, they rejoiced in his courage and willingness to share. They saw the best in him. They saw a man who was telling the truth. They saw a man who didn't want to stay in the place where he had been stuck.

Marianne was amazed by the things that her husband shared. Things she had no idea that he had experienced. Suddenly he began to become so very real to her. No longer an image of a husband, but flesh and blood, beating heart, feelings and experiences. He was so alive! And she was also amazed as she watched this small group of mature, loving Christians as they accepted him and honored his story.

The truth shall set you free. Not only the truth of who Jesus is, but also the truth of your own life. The path is not always straight or easy. Honestly, it is hardly ever easy! Obstacles and challenges make us who we are. And love rejoices in this truth.

PRAYER:

Dear God, I want to tell the truth. Release me from my fears and show me the way to be free. In Jesus name, Amen.

20

"*It* bears all things."

(1 Corinthians 13)

Marianne and her husband decided to begin again. Not as married people (although they did not get divorced). No, they chose a rather unique and creative path. They started dating each other. Marianne stayed at her parent's house for almost a year and they dated. At first they would go out once or twice a week and then they started talking on the phone. They even wrote letters to each other. They got to know each other in a very real way.

Marianne's parents were skeptical at first but they began to understand the purpose of this path. It was a time of discernment and a way for this young couple to find peace. Whether they continued their marriage or ended it, they were choosing a path that would make that decision a peaceful and loving decision.

There are times when marriages need to end. Sometimes a relationship is simply too unhealthy or burdened to ever be healed. It is not always a matter of having enough faith or love, sometimes the choice to marry was a mistake.

We make mistakes. There is no reason to continue that error every day of your life! Is there a biblical basis for this? I think so. Jesus came that we might have life and have it in abundance. He suffered and died so that we don't have to.

We are not here to suffer. We are not here to be martyrs to a bad marriage. We do need to try with everything we've got in us to make our marriages work but there are some situations in which it's just the wrong choice of partner.

But we can make the choice to divorce a loving decision. Divorce does not have to be an angry storm of, "It was all your fault!" and "I hate you!" No, I believe that Christians can approach divorce with agape love, that which bears all things, even the heartbreak of separation.

Love bears all things. Under our feet is the solid ground of God's love for us in all times and in all places. No matter what happens. If we are standing on that ground we can offer that kind of love to those in our lives. Even to those with whom we are in painful situations.

I can't tell you the end of the story. It isn't over yet. The decision isn't made. The process is ongoing. But I can tell you that for Marianne and her husband it had been a path that is hard, but supported with love from family, church, God and each other. And the love that they have found in them, and around them, has carried them through what might have been a nightmare, but instead has become one of the most profound and deeply instructive times of their lives.

PRAYER:

Dear God, I know that your peace can pass all my understanding. I need that. I need you to fill me with hope when I am hopeless. To bear my burdens when I am down. To send me companions for the journey. Thank you. In Jesus name, Amen.

21

"*B*elieves all things."

(1 Corinthians 13)

Last week a woman in my church read 1 Corinthians 13 from the pulpit. She is a petite woman, of about 40 who looks 60. She's been a very serious drug addict for the past 20 years and is trying, once again, to stay sober. She's missing most of her teeth. Her face is deeply lined and she is very thin. Two people stood behind her, her boyfriend and his daughter. She has tried and failed so many times before. This time, and it has been almost nine months now, she says something is different. She's not sure what "it" is. But something has changed.

"I don't feel like it's me doing it this time. I feel like God is doing it for me," she told me one day.

When I asked her to read scripture she refused.

"Oh no. I couldn't do that. Stand up there in front of all those people. No. They don't want to be looking at me! I don't belong there," she backed away from me.

I didn't ask again for several months. Again she refused. But now, nine months of sobriety have begun to affect her in a deep way. This time when I asked she hesitated.

"You could have your family up there with you, right behind you," I pointed out.

"Yeah?"

"Sure!"

She agreed to try. She practiced all week. And then Sunday morning there she was. She walked up to the pulpit and took a deep breath. And she read the whole thing. Straight through.

When she got to the part "love bears all things, believes all things, hopes all things, endures all things," I realized that tears were running down my face. I looked at her and understood that love had been with her through it all. What a life to bear – the addiction – the empty losing sadness of it all – the shame and the waste time – and through it all, love believed in her, bore her up, hoped for her and endured with her.

Unconditional. How impossible it is for us to accept this kind of love – a love that is not given only when we are good. No, it is not impossible, actually, but it is easy to turn away.

Her turning to us, reading the words of hope, her witness was the sermon of the day, the message, and the light in the darkness. Love believes all things, even when we have fallen.

PRAYER:

Dear God, Thank you for the light you constantly shine in my life. Help me to walk in your light, to stay in your hope and your unconditional love. In Jesus name, Amen.

22

"*Hopes* all things."

(1 Corinthians 13)

The bride is 23. She is tall and thin and she has long brown hair that cascades over her shoulders and down her white gown. The groom is 25 and almost her exact height. He has brown hair also, and he is smiling almost too broadly. I worry he may faint with happiness.

She is walking down the aisle. Her father walks with her. Everyone is standing. The music is playing – the "Here comes the bride" standard. I look at the faces of the congregation. They are shining, some people are crying.

We stand at the altar, this young couple looking like Adam and Eve, holding each others' hands for dear life, repeating the ancient vow, "To have and to hold, for better for worse, for richer for poorer, in sickness and in health …"

As I lead them in the wedding vows I glance up and see so many people looking intently, some tragically, some with joy, some with wonder, at this young couple.

Some are remembering the moment they said these vows and they are holding tightly to their spouse's hand, happily reliving the moment of their own marriage. Some are weeping as they think of the spouse that left them, and they remember a certain moment of their marriage and wonder how everything went so wrong. Others never had the chance to marry and wonder what it might have been like. Some feel grief for a spouse who has died and remember that moment long ago when they said their vows.

But the overall feeling in the sanctuary is hope. Even those who have experienced divorce or the death of a spouse feel hope for this young couple. No one stands up and shouts "Don't do it! You might get hurt!" There is a communal belief that it is worth the risk. Hope springs eternal.

Love is in the room. Love is in its most shiny form – youth – white dress – everyone clean and smooth – flowers – order and ritual – solid ground. Love is spinning like a young ballerina, showing off.

Eros. The desire of one for another. To touch and to have and to hold.

The love between this Adam and this Eve is intense and it is erotic and it is, most of us know, transitory. But our hope is that under the Eros, the beginning, are the other forms of love. Friendship, family and ultimately agape – that love which is not shiny but which is indestructible. It's the love that is the ground we can walk on; our own sturdy landscape.

PRAYER:

Dear God, In my life, in my marriage, I ask that all forms of love might find a place. The love of beginnings, the love of friendship, and most of all I ask for that solid ground upon which my marriage can live. I ask for agape love, the love that hopes all things. In Jesus name, Amen.

23

"Endures all things."

(1 Corinthians 13)

He's on the cross.

He endures for us that which a divine being does not need to experience. It was God's choice to endure suffering, to enter into human life and to feel as we feel, to hurt as we hurt, to experience the injustice and cruelty of this world.

He's on the cross. He understands. He even despairs with us. "My God, my God, why have you forsaken me?"

He could have come down. He could have ascended into heaven. But he stayed. He stayed and he endured because he chose to.

He chose to be with us.

I am not a Roman Catholic so most of my life I have worshiped the empty cross. For Protestant believers, the empty cross is the sign that Jesus was victorious over the cross. The cross could not hold him, God did not forsake him, he was and is the eternal Savior.

But there was a time, a sad time in my life, when I happened to wander into a church that had a life size crucifix – Christ hanging on the cross. It was a modern work of art. It was very realistic and Christ was suffering.

I looked up at him.

"You know. You know what I am going through, Jesus," I said to him.

And I felt that he was showing me that he could endure his own suffering, and that he could help me endure mine.

Because he didn't stay on the cross. This too shall pass, I thought, looking up at the crucified Christ. Weeping may last for the night but joy comes in the morning.

We have times in our lives, in our marriages, where there is very real suffering. We must and we can endure it. I have done it. I have seen many people endure. Christ endured the cross.

It doesn't last forever. You can, and you will endure whatever suffering is coming your way. Better days will come.

PRAYER:

Dear God, These days are hard. So hard. It seems that my pain will never end. Help me endure, help me hold on to hope and believe that better days are coming. In Jesus name, Amen.

(1 Corinthians 13)

Our individual lives will end. Our marriages will end. Our church buildings will someday fall down. Nations and principalities all come to an end.

Cheerful, huh?

Well, the point is, we have to look to the things eternal. What doesn't end? What shall we depend upon? What river shall we set our boat on and be taken away by?

Love never ends.

The love between individuals does end – at least in its earthly phase. But love itself, the power, the energy of love, does not end.

It is the river upon which, if we are courageous enough, our little lives can depend. It is the power that takes us farther than we might ever have imagined going.

And I believe that if we will place our hopes and dreams on this river, this love, that when our little lives end that we will become part of the river itself. And in that way, we also will never end.

Christ calls us to follow him. Where does he lead us?

He leads us on the journey, a journey of love and compassion. It takes us places we never could have reached on our own two legs.

He leads us to trust love.

The great thing to remember in marriage is that we don't generate the river. We only build the boat and get in it. Yes, there is some steering, some hanging on for dear life through the rapids, some bailing water out of the boat, some fishing, some laying back with our feet up while the current takes us – but we are not responsible for the power which bears us along.

This is a path that is worth committing to; the path of love.

It never ends.

As for political parties, they will end.

As for social networking sites, they will end.

As for fashion trends, they will end.

As for the latest how-to movement, it will end.

As for intellectual and cultural trends, they will end.

What does not end?

Love.

So drag your boat off the boring old shore and let love bear you and your marriage and your family and your heart and your dreams and your mind and your strength along its merry and winding way. Surrender to that which never ends.

PRAYER:

Dear God, Bear me along on your power, your river. I surrender to love, love that never ends. In Jesus name, Amen.

25

> "You have made my heart beat faster, my woman, my bride;
>
> You have made my heart beat faster with a single glance of your eyes,
>
> With a single strand of your necklace.
>
> How beautiful is your love, my woman, my bride!"
>
> (Song of Solomon 4:9)

And now back to sex.

Sexual intimacy can be such a wonderful thing. It is good for our bodies and for our hearts and our minds. The fact that God created us with the potential to enjoy sexual intimacy so much is not simply because it is procreative, but because it is a gift that enhances the relationship between two people.

Our culture has stolen much of the joy of sex and made it common, tawdry and even mundane.

The truth of the matter is that sex between two people who love each other, who are committed and in a healthy relationship, is a wonderful thing.

It makes our hearts beat faster. Oh, to be so connected to someone so much that the glance of their eyes can make our hearts beat faster!

Why does this get lost in marriage, this wonder and awe of each other?

Frankly, I think it comes from repressing our sexual life with each other. Sex becomes a tool, a way to push and sometimes even punish our spouse. Withholding becomes a way to express our anger. We don't make time to work through sexual tensions and to make this part of our life a priority.

Think of the time and energy people who are falling in love put into the romantic relationship. No wonder it is so great!

The honeymoon can't go on? Why not? It doesn't go on if you don't give your intimate and sexual relationship any time. Like a garden that never gets weeded or tended to, it will grow over and you can't even find it! But if you tend the garden and enlarge the garden and spend time – it can continue to be a wonderful place.

But it takes time. And energy. But it is worth it. A marriage with a happy, healthy and robust sexual intimacy is going to be so much stronger than a marriage that has no sexual joy.

PRAYER:

Dear God, Give me the courage to make time for romance and sexual intimacy with my spouse. Help me to make it a priority. In Jesus name, Amen.

26

"**How much better is your love than wine,**

And the fragrance of your oils

Than all kinds of spices!"

(Song of Solomon 4)

Wine creates an altered perception. It has an actual chemical effect on your brain. So does sex. And frankly, sex with your beloved spouse is a thousand times better for your health than a bottle of wine.

We are sensual beings. We feel, smell, taste, and hear – we are made for physical pleasures. Some pleasures take our energy and our soul away. Sex with your spouse doesn't. It gives energy, feeds your soul, and offers pleasures that are life-giving!

We often seek an altered perception. There are many layers to reality. We go to worship services to find a different way of looking at our lives. We pray to find an altered perception. There are many paths to a shift in thinking, feeling and knowing. The Christian realizes that we have a choice about the path we choose when seeking deeper experience.

Drugs, alcohol, and other addictive behavior are, frankly, effective ways to have a different life experience. But the price is dear. Our physical, emotional and spiritual health all pay a toll when we take the artificially induced road. Jesus calls us to see life differently – to see it with the eyes of love and compassion. Jesus calls us to walk a path that is deeper and richer, where our perception is constantly being altered. But it is a path that requires sobriety.

On the path of Christ there are great moments of ecstasy – spiritual enlightenment, intellectual epiphany and yes, physical pleasure. The pleasures of the flesh can lead to darkness, but not if they are experienced within a context of love and faithfulness. A good, healthy marriage, full of honesty and support, is a place to experience physical and sexual ecstasy. In this context, sexual joy adds to our love of life and our love of God. It is the fragrance and spice of life!

PRAYER:

Dear God, Help me to turn away from artificial joy and sensuality. Help me to find sexual joy within the bounds of a healthy relationship. In Jesus name, Amen.

27

> *"Therefore I say to you, do not worry about your life, what you will eat or what you will drink; nor about your body, what you will put on."*
>
> (Matthew 6)

"I'm worried that we aren't happy enough."

"I'm worried that I won't go to heaven."

"I'm worried that my husband won't go to heaven."

"I'm worried that my wife worries to much."

Worrying is such a spiraling, all-encompassing, serious, idiotic, whirling waste of time. And yet I find myself lost in it so often. You too?

What if? What if? What if????

"Do not worry about your life," says Jesus.

I answer, "But you didn't have kids! You didn't have to pay health insurance premiums! You didn't worry that you weighed too much or that your hair was turning gray! I worry that my husband doesn't love me enough. I worry that I will get cancer and die."

I worry because I think if I think about things enough maybe I can control them. And if I can control them, then I can make things go my way.

And that right there – those words – "MY WAY" are the core of the problem.

This life is not about *my way*. This is God's world. And frankly, when I get really honest, that is a relief. I might pretend that I know how things should go, but the truth is I don't know. I don't see the bigger picture. And neither do you.

If it were up to me, I would avoid all problems, all pain and all struggle in life a.nd in marriage. Yet most of my own personal and spiritual growth in my life and in marriage has come from struggle. The strongest Christians I know are usually people who have experienced great tragedy and challenges in life. And strong marriages grow from conflict and challenge.

Worrying is only the spinning of my own fear.

It may be an old tired motto by now but it works: Let go and let God.

PRAYER:

Dear God, I am so thankful that you are in charge. What a relief. Into your power I commend my spirit, my life, what I will eat and what I will wear, and all the things that happen to me in this coming day. I am yours. Use me as you will. In Jesus name, Amen.

28

"Look at the birds of the air, for they neither sow nor reap nor gather into barns; yet your heavenly Father feeds them. Consider the lilies of the field, how they grow: they neither toil nor spin; and yet I say to you that even Solomon in all his glory was not arrayed like one of these. Now if God so clothes the grass of the field, which today is, and tomorrow is thrown into the oven, will He not much more clothe you, O you of little faith."

(Matthew 6)

Sister Wendy, a Roman Catholic nun and art critic, once said, "I have no faith. I never had any doubt, therefore I never needed any faith."

That does not describe me. Nor most of the people I know. Yes, I've known a few pure souls who seemed born with a kind of deep innocence that never left them. But most of us roll around in the mud wrestling with angels, devils and ourselves!

Doubt is my close companion. It's always at my elbow.

Therefore I need a great deal of faith.

Especially when it comes to marriage and intimate love. All around us marriages fall apart. Our parents, our friends, and many of us have had the experience of going through our own divorce or our children's divorces. Our culture is steeped in the experience of marriages falling apart.

Yes, the birds get spectacular feathers and the lilies gleam white in the sunlight, but what about all those lonely people? I look around and wonder, "Where is God in all this sadness?"

It is in the sadness and loneliness of my own life that I lean on my other companion, faith. Faith is that great armchair I crawl into when I don't know where else to go. The chair is soft and it is well worn. It is the place where I don't have to know why things are the way they are.

In relationships there are many times when we simply don't know what to do. We don't know what to say or how to fix a situation. These are the times to crawl into the armchair of faith and let go.

Jesus says that his burden is light and if we go to him, we will find rest for our soul.

Jesus is my armchair. And when I am done resting, I go back to the world and keep at it. Which is all I am asked to do. Like a bird in the air, like a lily in the field, we all need to rest. Give it a rest.

PRAYER:

Dear God, Sometimes I simply am at a loss. I don't know what to do. This is one of those times. Can I come to you? Will you hold me until my doubt and fear passes? Hold me Lord, and let me rest. In Jesus name, Amen.

29

"Therefore do not worry, saying, 'What shall we eat?' or 'What shall we drink?' or 'What shall we wear?' For after all these things the Gentiles seek. For your heavenly Father knows that you need all these things. But seek first the kingdom of God and His righteousness, and all these things shall be added to you. Therefore do not worry about tomorrow, for tomorrow will worry about its own things. Sufficient for the day is its own trouble.

(Matthew 6)

Be in the moment. What else is there?

Margaret was 75 when I first met her. Her forehead was smooth but she had deep laugh lines flowing out from her bright green eyes and lining her wide, smiling mouth. She was rarely without a smile.

"A Christian should have a hair trigger laugh!" she would say to me. Her laugh was big, and lasted a long time. She was a knee slapper and a back patter.

Margaret had grown up in the same small town she still lived in. She hadn't traveled much, hadn't been to college, didn't read much, never held a "fancy" job (as she put it) and yet she struck me as one of the more sophisticated, wise women I'd ever met. She was someone that everyone wanted around. She made the world a better place simply by being in the vicinity.

Margaret had a way of being in the moment. She didn't like making plans. We'd have a church meeting and when things got too organized she'd lean back in her chair and let out a big snore. And then she'd laugh. We'd all laugh.

"Who knows what we'll be doing next year!" she'd say. "Give it a rest!"

Her husband, Van, was probably the healthiest man of his age I've ever met. He was the quintessential outdoorsman. Always out on the lake, fishing, or in the woods, hunting or tracking for hunting season. He had the same "seize the day" joy that his wife did. They lived very simply. Their tiny ranch house wasn't much to crow about and they generally had the kind of cars that you weren't sure were going to make it home. They had a son who turned out pretty well and moved a few doors down. They were a tight family. They actually liked spending time together.

I would say that they sought the kingdom of God first. They put a high value on the moment and making sure that love was in the air. They didn't wear their religion like a campaign button, but rather it was a seamless part of their life. They loved. They lived with dignity. They loved each other and the world they found themselves in.

Were there problems? Sure. But not extra ones. Not tomorrow's problems, and not yesterday's – only the one in the moment.

PRAYER:

**Dear God, This is the day that you have made.
Give me the peace and strength to find joy in it.
Keep my mind here. In Jesus name, Amen.**

30

"Do not lay up for yourselves treasures on earth, where moth and rust destroy and where thieves break in and steal, but lay up for yourselves treasures in heaven, where neither moth nor rust destroys and where thieves do not break in and steal. For where your treasure is, there your heart will be also."

(Matthew 6)

What do you treasure? What is of the greatest value in your life?

Do you treasure your spouse?

The principle of investment is important in marriage. The more you invest in your marriage and in your husband or wife, the more your treasure will abide there.

She comes clomping in the front door of the church. The bitter winter wind slams the door behind her. She turns.

"Oh dear," she mutters. "What to do?" Her hands are full. She carries a platter of muffins, covered with plastic wrap. She looks back at the door. "Here," she says handing me the muffins.

The wind is rattling the front door. She is there. Opening the door as he enters. His arms are heavy with several platters and a basket. He staggers in, shoved by winter, a burst of snow flying around his head and shoulders.

"Here!" she slams the door firmly shut behind her husband and grabs one of the platters. They stamp their feet and then slowly walk across the vestibule toward the fellowship hall.

They are providing for coffee hour today. She spent most of Saturday baking. In they go, down past the tables and into the kitchen. They make another trip. This time I help them.

Walking behind them I see how they each are scanning the world for the other. Is the ice too slippery for her? He holds his hand out. Are the steps too snowy for him? She waits at the foot of the stairs for him to come down. Together they walk, in step with each other, across the driveway and to their car. I follow, bending in against a hard-handed wind.

They have a routine. They don't speak. He opens the door. She hands him the platters and a bag of something or other. He takes it and then she pulls out one more box and closes the door with her ample hip. I try to help but they don't seem to need me. I follow dutifully. Learning.

They have spent 40 years together; investing in each other; learning the patterns, the needs, the sight and smell, the instinct, the fears and the thoughts of each other. Now their investment pays off in seamless, peaceful days. Their treasure is each other. And therein lies their heart. Oh, to be so strong. So simple.

PRAYER:

Dear God, Change my heart, O God. Mold me, casting away all that is unnecessary. Teach me to love. In Jesus name, Amen.

31

"*I* am the rose of Sharon, and the lily of the valleys. As the lily among thorns, so is my love among the daughters. As the apple tree among the trees of the wood, so is my beloved among the sons. I sat down under his shadow with great delight, and his fruit was sweet to my taste. He brought me to the banqueting house, and his banner over me was love."

(Song of Solomon: Chapter 2)

Oh, young love. It's found in people of all ages. When intimate love is born it begins life as a scarlet flower blooming sticky with scent, the dawn sun rising bright and hot, full moons shining and it feels like an endless fall into the sea. It is bliss.

It will come and go throughout marriage – if we let it. Often we push it away. It makes us so vulnerable, so naked.

The thrill of being loved so completely gives us courage when a relationship begins. We are so emboldened by the power of his look, her smile or his touch, that we forget ourselves. We forget our shame. We are Adam and Eve wandering around the Garden of Eden and we don't need anything to hide behind because love is enough.

But then life happens. And we find our hearts torn apart by this man, and our ego destroyed by this woman and we begin to seek cover. We are ashamed. We are frightened. And the love that floats and comes when it will, the Holy Spirit of love that flits like a hummingbird through the blooming of our life, cannot find us. We are hiding deep in shadow. We are running from the garden. We dig ourselves into the dirt. Down. Down. We seek safety.

His banner over me was love.

I was the Rose of Sharon.

Was.

And now, in the midst of marriage? Can we find the courage to take off our armor and meet again under the full moon? When is the last time you and your spouse lay in the wet grass of a summer's dawn and kissed for half an hour before coming up for air? When did you gaze at one another, memorizing the lines and colors of your lover's face? How did you forget to do such things? Is there a way back to the garden? Can the hummingbird find you?

Young love doesn't know the cost. Once we know the cost, and how much it can sting, how much it can wound, we back off. We run.

There are other gates that lead us back to the garden. Perhaps we have grown too old or too cynical to use the main gate – to cast off all our clothing and run in with abandon. But there are other gates – gates that are more gentle, more subtle. And yet still lead us to bliss.

Look for them. Find them. Open them. Come back.

PRAYER:

Dear God, I want to love again. To feel, at least now and then, the bliss of the love I felt in those first weeks and months. Show me the way, O God. Show me the gate through which I can enter in again. In Jesus name, Amen.

32

(Take One)
"Stay me with flagons, comfort me with apples: for I am sick with love."

(Song of Solomon: Chapter 2)

The other gates. The alternative entrances to the blessed Garden of Eden? Is there a side door?

When we are first in love and flush with the sickness that is both bliss and anxiety, we have no shame. Love is all there is. He is. She is. We think of them all day. We wake with them on our mind. If there is a door in to the garden of love we will kick it open if necessary. No shame.

But when we grow older in love and are more self-conscious, we lose our freedom. We are suddenly more apprehensive about approaching our beloved. It all becomes ordinary. To show or even to feel intense affection for our spouse can sometimes make us feel embarrassed, too vulnerable.

"I'd just feel silly if I got all romantic with my husband," she says to me. "He's just Albert. There's nothing really interesting about him. Nothing to get too blissful about." She laughs and rolls her eyes.

"How did you feel about him at the beginning of your relationship?" I ask.

"Oh, who can think back that far? I don't know," she says, evading my question.

"Think back," I say pushing her to remember.

"Well, of course I thought he was sweet. Handsome. He was ... you know how it is when it all begins. I had a lot of silly thoughts in my head," she pauses. Then I notice that she starts to smile. "Albert. Huh. Yes. He was actually something."

"And what is he now?"

She looks up at me and to my surprise her eyes fill with tears.

"What is it?" I question her.

"I guess I realize that he is still something. I just had this feeling about how much I still like him," she smiled.

One of the gates to the garden is memory; remembering, mulling over, looking back to those early times. Spend some time together looking at pictures of those early days, reading any letters or diaries that you have. Talking about what you remember of each other in the early weeks, months and even years of your life together – a gentle gate into the garden.

PRAYER:

Dear God, As I look back, I remember the early feelings I had for my spouse. I remember how I felt. Help me to find that feeling in me now, in my daily life with him/her. Help me to find the gate into the garden. In Jesus name, Amen.

33

(Take Two)
"Stay me with flagons, comfort me with apples: for I am sick with love."

(Song of Solomon: Chapter 2)

One gate takes us back to the past, another to the future. Comfort me with apples. I am sick with love. Oh, the pain that love brings. The anxiety that we might lose the person we love.

One of the doors into the garden is to face the fact that life is fragile. We are, all of us, only passing through. There will be a time when your beloved will no longer be with you. And comfort will be hard to find. We take our spouses for granted. We forget to feel the temporary state of life.

When we first fall in love, this anxiety about the potential loss of the one we are in love with is what it means to be sick with love. It is so good, so important, that the thought of losing him/her is painful. After the years pass, however, we assume that they are there, that they will always be there.

In one small church I served, the back row on the left side was filled with widows. They sat in a line, in solidarity almost, having passed into that time of life when death comes sweeping through all too easily. Their husbands were gone.

This too shall pass.

Sometimes getting in touch with the reality that we are all here for a limited time helps us seize the day.

What do the dying say? Do they wish they had washed the car more often? Do they regret that they should have worked longer hours? No. What comes clear when death looms is that love and the people that we love are all that matters.

Tell them that you love them, the dying advise. Tell them now.

Whatever it takes to wake you (and me) up from our stupor, from our shame, from our reluctance to be vulnerable to our spouse – whatever it takes – go there!!!

Life is short.

"I should have told her," he says to me. We are staying at the graveside, waiting for the hearse. "I should have told her," he says it again, quietly.

"What?" I say, knowing already what he is going to say," What should you have told her?"

"That I loved her," he chokes as he speaks and puts his hand over his mouth.

I want to comfort him. I want to tell him that she knew. I want him to feel better. But the truth is, he should have told her.

So I am telling you. I am passing on the hard-earned wisdom that he whispered that spring afternoon under the warm sun, looking down at his wife's grave.

Take what gate you must. Be it past or future. Tell her. Hold him. There is nothing to be ashamed of. Come in through any door you can find. Come in.

PRAYER:

Dear God, Wake me up, O God! Life is short. Whatever it takes, I want back into the life and love of my marriage. Give me courage and take away my shame. In Jesus name I pray, Amen.

34

"His left hand is under my head, and his right hand doth embrace me."

(Song of Solomon: Chapter 2)

Affection in marriage. How much we touched each other when we were dating! He always held my hand. She always stroked my face. He couldn't sit by me without touching me!

We smile when we see older couples holding hands. Why? Because it isn't that common. All too soon in marriage affection can lessen. We get distracted with the other things in life.

Affection is actually good for one's health. There are studies that show how blood pressure drops after an affectionate touch from one's spouse.

Look carefully at the scripture: "His left hand is under my head and his right hand doth embrace me." This is all encompassing – his arms are around me, one under my head and the other wrapped around my body. What does that say?

It says, "I want to wrap my self around you. I want to feel you. I want you."

This kind of affection is only given by our intimate partner. Why do we so often withhold it when in fact it is life-giving? Jogging, yes ... there are benefits, but they pale in comparison to the left hand under your head and the right hand embracing you. And how easy is affection?

Keeping a body healthy means making good choices all day long. The same is true with marriage. Think of your marriage as a living entity. It needs to be fed, it needs to be touched with affection and love, it needs space, it needs care.

For couples that are working their way back to a healthy relationship, affection is important. Through small touches, throughout the day, an atmosphere of support and care can be created. Affection is action.

Arguments? Let them be softened with the touch of a hand. Put your hand on her back. Smooth her hair from her face. Put your hand on his shoulder. Slip your hand into his.

"Sometimes we don't know what to say to each other. We get to this awkward moment. I don't want to apologize. I'm not wrong! But I don't want to be mad at him. So I will just go over and stand near him. Maybe lean in a little bit. Squeeze his hand or something. That breaks the ice. And then ... it gets all better," she nods, remembering with pleasure how affection helps her and her husband get through little problems. She's been married three decades.

It's the little things.

PRAYER:

Dear God, I want a healthy marriage. Help me to care for what lives between us with affection. Help me to remember to reach out, physically, and connect with my spouse. In Jesus name, Amen.

35

"My beloved spake, and said unto me, Rise up, my love, my fair one, and come away. For, lo, the winter is past, the rain is over and gone; The flowers appear on the earth; the time of the singing of birds is come, and the voice of the turtledove is heard in our land; The fig tree putteth forth her green figs, and the vines with the tender grape give a good smell. Arise, my love, my fair one, and come away."

(Song of Solomon: Chapter 2)

Oh if only our beloved husband would say to us, "Rise up, my love, my fair one, and come away." Probably not going to happen.

Oh, if only the wife said, "Lo! The winter is past and the rain is over and gone."

No, we tend to grunt at each other. "Hey you. Over here."

One of the great things about the King James Version of the Bible is that it was translated during a time when poetry was deeply woven into the daily speech patterns of people. Conversation was an art form. Shakespeare wrote during this period! There were no televisions or newspaper or texting or emailing to distract from the primary form of communication: conversation. There are other versions of the Bible that are more helpful when engaged in serious study, but there is nothing like the KJV to uplift the heart.

If a couple studies the Bible together, especially if they are studying the Song of Solomon or the Psalms, using the poetic KJV is highly recommended. Read out loud! Let the beautiful phrases become part of our conversation with each other – even if it is in a funny way.

Tomorrow morning, instead of grunting, "Hey get up, Lazy Bones!" try whispering, "Arise my love, my fair one, and come away." No doubt you will be greeted with a smile, maybe even a good hearty laugh, as opposed to a pillow directed at your head.

The deeper lesson is that what we say to each other matters – both the substance of our speech but also the form of it. One of the reasons Christians generally (!) don't swear is that cursing makes our conversation so ugly. Conversation can be an art form again. Perhaps not in the flowery style of the KJV Song of Solomon, but in its own way, conversation can be rich and full.

PRAYER:

Dear God, My words are important and so I ask that you might inspire me to speak well, to speak with dignity, humor and beauty. Inspire me to happy poetic heights! In Jesus name, Amen.

36

"Take us the foxes, the little foxes, that spoil the vines: for our vines have tender grapes."

(Song of Solomon: Chapter 2)

What an odd little line this is! Foxes that steal the precious grapes.

It is a line about protection. Love, marriage and relationships need protection. There are foxes that want to steal that which is precious. Every marriage has its little foxes – foxy predators who circle around and spoil that which is precious.

What is precious in your marriage? There are the obvious jewels – fidelity, honesty, shared faith in God and in marriage itself. Those are at the center of every marriage.

We protect these jewels through vigilance – daily, hourly, moment-by-moment vigilance of the things we say and do. We protect them through prayer, worship, being part of a Christian community, and in the relationship that we have with God as we know him in Christ.

But in your own marriage what is it that you value?

"When we first dated we went dancing all the time. Now we never go."

"When we first dated we sang together. We were in the choir. We used to sit for hours at the piano and sing duets. Now, we just don't have time."

"The first thing that attracted me to him was how smooth he was on the ice. He could skate like the wind! Wow. I don't think we've gone skating for a decade. We just stopped. Sometimes he would go with the kids but the two of us never go."

Well, for heaven's sake – do the stuff you like to do! Make a list. Talk about what makes you happy. What did you do at the beginning of your relationship that you stopped doing? Don't worry about why you stopped – just see if you can find a way to start again.

Tender grapes.

Each marriage has jewels, things that are precious between the two of you. Don't let them get lost in the rush of life. Protect them. Keep the little foxes out.

PRAYER:

Dear God, First, help me remember what is precious in my marriage! Then give me the strength to protect the grapes, to keep the jewels of my marriage intact and shining. Help me chase away the foxes. In Jesus name, Amen.

37

"**My beloved is mine, and I am his: he feedeth among the lilies. Until the daybreak, and the shadows flee away, turn, my beloved, and be thou like a roe or a young hart upon the mountains of Bether.**"

(Song of Solomon: Chapter 2)

My beloved is mine. Really? That's how it feels. The truth is – we belong to God, and hopefully to ourselves. No human can possess us. Not even the one who has loved us for so long. Not our parents, not our children, not our husbands and not our wives. We belong to God.

The fun of love, the thrill of it, is that we choose to give ourselves to others. If we were mere possessions, there would be no giving. No surrender. No choice to love.

"I just can't believe he likes me as much as I like him," the young woman says, beaming from the inside out, beaming with wonder.

She had been in love for about six months. They were still in that gazing stage – gazing for hours at his eyes, her nose, his mouth, her shoulders, watching every move, feeding among the lilies. The Song of Solomon sings of that gazing stage when it almost feels as if the beloved belongs to oneself. That is some of the grief when love starts to mature.

He's got a mind of his own? What?

She wasn't like that before ... who is this?

Give up the ownership. Give it up before it starts. Connected? Yes. But not bought and paid for. Ownership is fairly boring, frankly. "She loves me because I own her." Huh? Try that next to – "She loves me of her own free will, and I don't know why! She loves me!" said the young man who had become the focus of the young woman (mentioned above) and her passion. How could someone so beautiful love him so much? He never thought a girl like this would think he was the one!

I sat with them, two young people in their early 20s, brimming with the confidence that comes from being loved so boldly, and we planned their wedding. The air was charged with longing as they leaned into each other. Hands entwined. They could barely look away from the other. I had a hard time keeping their attention.

There was a voice in me that said, "Tell them it won't last ..." but I did not tell them. They would find out soon enough that love matures and hurts and gets even better. But for now, why not let them swim in the warm waters of wonder? The waters were shallow and shining, and they were together.

Enjoy, I thought to myself. I wanted to shake them and yell "Enjoy it now!!! Seize the day!!! Don't mess it up!!" But I didn't do that either. I let them be – lost in the world of new love. They were doing fine. Longing, but not belonging.

PRAYER:

Dear God, I belong to you. Stir up my longing for my spouse. Let me seize the day. In Jesus name, Amen.

38

"For I am convinced that neither death nor life, neither angels nor demons, neither the present nor the future, nor any powers, neither height nor depth, nor anything else in all creation, will be able to separate us from the love of God that is in Christ Jesus our Lord."

(Romans 8:39-39)

This is my favorite verse in the Bible. It is the solid ground that my life is built on. Nothing will be able to separate me, or you, from the love of God that is in Christ Jesus. When I face fears, whether they are the fear of the dark, death or divorce, my heart becomes calm when I think on this scripture.

Many things will happen in this life. Storms roll through. Glass breaks. Lightning strikes. People change. In the ever-changing landscape of being a human, I need some place to stand where am not thrown by the tides of fortune. The love of God is unshakable. At least it has always felt so in my life. At the very worst of times, God is there with me. At the very best of times, still there. When things get boring, yup, not moving. Still there. There. Here. With me.

If I didn't have this place to live my life from, I would feel so helpless. How do people do it that have no sense of God's love for them? How blessed I have been to have the experience and the words to describe that experience given to me in my life!

There was a couple that came in to see me who did not have solid ground. Their panic was palpable. They were so frightened at the thought of their marriage failing that they couldn't even talk about what the problem was. When I inquired about what their situation was, they were unable to speak. Then they started to cry. Then they left. I watched them go, stumbling out to the car, afraid to look at each other.

They came back several times but were never able to talk about their struggle. They talked lightly and briefly about how they didn't want to be part of any "religion" because churches were so hypocritical. (I had to smile, wondering why they had come to see me in the first place. Maybe because I am cheap. Well, free.) They showed me pictures of their house and their boat. But when I would push them into a real conversation, the silence built up like a great wall and then the tears spilled over and they were out the door.

Now, don't get me wrong, those of us who stand on the solid ground of God's love also cry quite a bit and are afraid of things and sometimes we run. But the love of God runs with us and eventually we remember that as long as we have God's love, the rest can be dealt with.

If you are facing difficulties in your marriage, ask yourself if you honestly have solid ground. If you don't, go find it. If you do, trust it. It is from this foundation that the difficulties of life can be seen in perspective.

PRAYER:

Dear God, You are the solid ground. Your love is eternal. It is what I need. It is all I need. Help me to trust you completely. In Jesus name, Amen.

39

"*I* tell you the truth, you will weep and mourn while the world rejoices. You will grieve, but your grief will turn to joy. A woman giving birth to a child has pain because her time has come; but when her baby is born she forgets the anguish because of her joy that a child is born into the world.

So with you: Now is your time of grief, but I will see you again and you will rejoice, and no one will take away your joy."

(John 16)

The disciples were afraid. They felt the time coming when Jesus would be taken from them. And then who would they be? What would happen to them? It would be the end of the world.

Marriages change. They are born and they grow and they change. The changes in marriage are often difficult. Like a baby being born. Change makes us feel afraid, often.

The disciples didn't want change.

Humans generally want things to be the same. Even if those things are dysfunctional, unhealthy or devoid of love. We get used to things and we so often cling to them out of fear.

Marriages are like children – at some point they get too big for the womb and they have to move into the next stage. A couple must birth the next stage of their marriage. I could list the stages but frankly, each marriage has its own stages. And often you aren't prepared for them. They come upon you and you have to work. You have to grieve. You have to bear the anguish of letting go of the marriage that was and giving birth to the marriage that needs to emerge.

"I just don't feel right," the husband said to me. "We're not like we used to be."

"So!" his wife snapped back. "I think that's a good thing. I'm tired of the way things were."

"What?" he looked stunned. "You never said. You seemed always happy. Were you lying to me?"

"No, I wasn't lying to you! I was okay with things but then I started growing up, wanting new things in my life. Can't I change? Can't I learn things and be different sometimes?" She spoke heatedly, as if these words had been building up steam for years. "What about me?"

"Well ... I don't know, I want you to be happy but ... frankly ... if you are different, if you change," he paused for a long moment and then quickly said, "maybe you won't want me anymore."

"Why would you think that?" she said, suddenly smiling.

"Why wouldn't I think that?" he said with exasperation.

"Oh. Oh my. My dear," she reached out to him and spoke with sudden tenderness, "I want you. I love you. That isn't changing. But I've got to find my own life. I'm not rejecting you, I'm just trying to find me."

PRAYER:

Dear God, You know the fears in my heart. I am facing changes in my life, in me, in my thinking and in the things I want to do. Give me the courage to allow your hands and your power to help me in this labor. In Jesus name, Amen.

40

"Now the body is not made up of one part but of many. If the foot should say, 'Because I am not a hand, I do not belong to the body,' it would not for that reason cease to be part of the body. And if the ear should say, 'Because I am not an eye, I do not belong to the body,' it would not for that reason cease to be part of the body. If the whole body were an eye, where would the sense of hearing be? If the whole body were an ear, where would the sense of smell be? But in fact God has arranged the parts in the body, every one of them, just as he wanted them to be. If they were all one part, where would the body be? As it is, there are many parts, but one body."

(1st Corinthians 12:14-20)

In this scripture Paul is referring to the church and using the imagery of the body to describe how many different people, different parts, each have a part to play in the larger body. The same imagery can be applied to marriage. Each partner has gifts, a part to play in the body of the marriage.

In traditional marriage, roles emerged for men and women based largely on biology and upon the structure of the society at the time. In our modern age much of the traditional structure has started to break down. This has offered more choice, more freedom and also, often, more confusion and heartbreak.

Maria was exhausted. She was working full time, raising three children, taking care of the domestic needs like cleaning and cooking, and she simply felt at the edge of her strength most of the time. Her husband also worked full time, was responsible for most of the "outside" tasks, cars, care of the home and yard, bills and such. They were both involved in church and several other community groups.

"I don't know if I can keep going," she told me. "Every morning I feel like if only I can get through this day, then I will be all right."

Her husband, Mark, agreed. "I feel the same way. Life is a blur. I don't want to live like this! It's like I'm running as fast as I can every day."

Modern life is stretching us thin.

This scripture came to mind as I listened to them. We got it out and read it together. We talked about ways they could simplify things and ways they could partner better so that the parts of the body might be different but work together.

I asked them to come up with a list of the things each of them was really good at. What are your gifts? What things in the day do you look forward to doing? When does time fly?

I'll continue with their story in the next devotion.

PRAYER:

Dear God, I get overwhelmed by my life some days. Help me focus on what I am good at, what my gifts are, what my strengths are. In Jesus name, Amen.

41

"*The* he eye cannot say to the hand, 'I don't need you!' And the head cannot say to the feet, 'I don't need you!'"

(1st Corinthians 12:21)

Maria and Mark began meeting with me on a regular basis and slowly they developed an understanding of what their individual gifts from God were. Surprisingly the list was a mix of traditional and non-traditional things. For instance, Mark felt his strongest gift was parenting. He loved spending time with his children. His greatest drain in life was the demanding job that he had. For Maria, she felt God's blessing on her when she was creating a true home for her family. She loved to nurture her family through creating beautiful spaces in her home and organizing special family events.

They began to look carefully at their finances and over several months they made some decisions to radically change their life for the better. They both began to work part time. Mark had to keep his hours fairly high to retain his benefits and Maria was able to work a mere 15 hours a week outside the home! They started spending much more time with their children, with each other and they stopped duplicating efforts.

Like the scripture, they allowed each other to fully take over in various areas. They had both been involved in so many of the daily tasks. Now, they simply chose and let the other person completely have decision-making power in whatever "part of the body" they were best at.

"I didn't realize how much I was interfering with her, telling her what to do all the time and trying to control situations that she was completely able to handle," Mark reported.

"We just simplified everything," Maria said with wonder, "and suddenly I have a life!"

"And a partner!" he smiled at her.

We can need each other in marriage but not duplicate or control each other. Modern life has us running all over the place, each of us doing everything. Simplify. Let the body be what it is. Every task is important but it doesn't need to get done twice!

Their health began to improve, their children started doing better in school, and life started being fun.

Jesus came that we might have life and have it in abundance. Simplify. Let go of the needless suffering.

PRAYER:

Dear God, Help me to need my spouse but not to control them. Help me to let go of that which drains me and to do the things that bring me life. Lead me Lord, In Jesus name, Amen.

42

> "If one part suffers, every part suffers with it; if one part is honored, every part rejoices with it."
>
> (1st Corinthians 12:26)

Love hurts. It hurts because when we are truly connected with someone, when we love and care for them, what affects them matters to us. It affects us also. Empathy is the connection of one person to another. We feel one another's pain and joy. This happens so deeply with our children but it also can, and should, happen with our spouse.

Often a partner will resist this connection because they don't want to feel the pain of their spouse. But to deny the suffering, one must deny the joy. There is only one door. The door is either open or shut. You can't open the door to happiness but not to pain. Sorry. But that's the way it is.

Remember that feelings are a river – they flow – they keep flowing on and new feelings come endlessly. Don't be too attached to the feelings. This too shall pass. Feel them and then let them move through you.

A relationship is so much more than feeling. It is a life together. Feeling is part of that life. Being empathetic and open to each other is part of staying connected. But the connection should not depend upon feeling good, nor should it be frightened off by feeling bad!

If you can develop a strong relationship, one based on friendship, honesty and integrity, the feelings will flow freely, without fear. You will feel sadness when your husband is struggling and you will feel joy when your wife is bounding around cheerfully! But mostly you will feel connected – no matter what – bonded beyond all feeling but not afraid of feeling.

The wonderful hymn, "Blest Be the Tie That Binds" (by John Fawcett, 1782) has this verse:

"We share each other's woes, our mutual burdens bear,

and often for each other flows the sympathizing tear."

If we step away from the painful parts of love, the sharing and bearing of burdens, then we also are absent for the ecstatic moments of oneness!

PRAYER:

Dear God, May I be blessed with the courage to open my heart to the one I love. In his sorrow, in her joy, let me be present. Let me not turn away, nor back off, but give me the strength to be there. In Jesus name, Amen.

43

"*The* wise woman builds her house, but with her own hands the foolish one tears hers down."

(Proverbs 14:1)

" He's just such a jerk. You wouldn't believe the things he says. He comes home from work and he just talks on and on about himself. Never asks about me. And his mother, oh my gosh, she's a nightmare. I don't know how my father-in-law puts up with her. Did you hear about his sister? She's gotten fired again from her job and I'm sure it is her own fault. My husband is just like her. They are both so lazy. I can't stand him anymore. Really. He drives me crazy. And he never thanks me for anything. I do so much and he hardly notices. He's not mature. He's a very immature person," she stopped and took a deep breath and started in again.

I sat and watched her prattle on. Her face was red. Her hands clenched in anger. She was working up to the climax.

"I can't stand him! Really. Don't you agree that he is just awful?" she looked up at me with big eyes. "Can you do something? Talk to him and tell him to change or something?"

She was tearing down her house. Tearing down her husband. She was seeing everything that was wrong with him and by focusing on it she was making him weaker and weaker.

Did I mention that her husband was seated next to her during this tirade?

I looked over at him. His face was shut. Blank. He was trying, successfully, not to be present.

We all have foolish moments – moments in which we tear down that which we live in: our own life, our love, our marriage. The foolish one tears down that which is hers.

What effect did this tirade have on him? It reinforced his weakness. It made him feel about two feet tall. It made him ashamed and he retreated. As he should have!

Should she have lied? Should she have covered up her feelings? No. But there is no need to indulge in negative feeling. Let it flow through you and move on. Wait until the positive comes along and then build up with wisdom that which is strong. Let the weak parts of your beloved fade from view. Do not drag them out and put a big spotlight on them and invite people over to view his/her weakness! What a waste of time.

She was tearing him down when her job as a wife and a friend and a partner was to build up that which is strong in him. And there was so much that was strong. There always is.

PRAYER:

Dear God, May I be blessed with the courage to open my heart to the one I love. In his sorrow, in her joy, let me be present. Let me not turn away, nor back off, but give me the strength to be there. In Jesus name, Amen.

44

"*A*gentle answer turns away wrath, but a harsh word stirs up anger."

(Proverbs 15:1)

She had been criticizing him for weeks now. At first he felt bad. Then he felt worse. And then he stopped feeling. His anger had spilled over to the point that it startled him. He shut down. He was there but not there.

How do we meet anger, even wrath, from our spouse? We all get angry from time to time. It is inevitable that even the most patient person will have a breaking point. Proverbs 15:1 reminds us that we have a choice.

He looked back at how he first reacted when she criticized him for his handling of their family finances. He had not paid several bills and now things were piling up. She was angry at his inattention, angry at his irresponsible behavior. She lost her temper with him when she found a disconnect notice from the electric company. His wife didn't yell very often. But here she was, standing in front of him, her voice loud and quivering with anger.

"What did you do when she was yelling at you?" I asked him.

"I yelled back. Man, I really let loose. I don't do that much but I guess I felt kind of guilty and instead of admitting it I got all defensive," he said sheepishly.

"Then what happened?"

"She started crying. She ran off and slammed the bedroom door and wouldn't speak to me for hours and when she did she was very cold. And she stayed that way. She's been mad at me for more than a month."

"Have you tried to make peace?"

There was a long pause. Finally he looked up and I was surprised to see such anger in his face. "No! It's not my fault. I'm not going to fix it!" he spoke with vehemence.

"Okay. Whose fault is it?"

"Hers."

"Un huh."

We sat in silence for a long time. His arms were crossed. He was leaning back in his chair, looking out the window. Finally he sighed deeply and dropped his head.

"You know that God loves you no matter what. You don't have to be perfect. You don't have to do everything right. And ultimately it doesn't matter whose fault it is. There is always a way through; a loving way. I believe you can find it," I spoke quietly.

He looked up at me with surprise. I felt a little surprised myself! Where had that come from? It was a moment of agape love in me – God coming through me – light in the darkness. As a human I was actually a little judgmental of him, and caught up in analyzing and criticizing. But then something happened in my own heart and I saw him as I think God might see him: as a child who is learning, a beautiful child with great potential to love and to be loved. The feeling in the room changed. I could see his body relax. I felt such pride in him suddenly, a pride that flowed through me, from some greater source.

"You are doing the best you can. Keep going. You will find your way," I said. And we both stood and he left, his head held high.

PRAYER:

Dear God, Help me believe that I am doing the best I can. May I feel your unconditional love for me and through me for others. In Jesus name, Amen.

45

> "The tongue that brings healing is a tree of life, but a deceitful tongue crushes the spirit."
>
> (Proverbs 15:4)

She lied.

It was a small lie. Nothing spectacular. Nothing truly devious. And yet it was a lie. She told one. And then she told another. It got easier. Soon she began to lie without even planning it. She would simply open her mouth and out came something that surprised even her.

"I would watch myself, seriously, and be stunned at the things I was saying. But then once they were said, I couldn't take them back. I had to keep going. Keep lying," she admitted to the group.

Finally, thanks be to God, she got caught. She was caught in a simple lie that she had told her husband about where she was going. Suddenly she had to pay the consequences. And with his help, and with the help of her small support group at church, she began to change. She began to tell the truth.

"It is such a relief. To not be thinking about how to get out of something or to try and remember what I lied about and when. I was so tense all the time, thinking I was about to be found out!" she laughed and we laughed with her.

The relief in her was so clear. Her whole body relaxed and her face was open and free with us all.

"You look like a different person," I noted.

"I look like myself," she said.

PRAYER:

Dear God, Help me believe that I am doing the best I can. May I feel your unconditional love for me and through me for others. In Jesus name, Amen.

46

"Draw near to God, and he will draw near to you."

(James 4:8)

When in doubt, go to God.

Funny that we so often run and hide from God when we are filled with doubts and fears. We've got this crazy notion that we have to be good in front of God, that we have to be impressive, dressed nice, thinking perfect thoughts and being wise. Well, guess what? God can see in the dark. God sees us when we are running away. God sees us hiding in the closet. God sees us when we are a mess.

So, since he's seeing us anyway, and evidently (according to Jesus) loving us, what is the point of hiding? When doubts and troubles come, when our marriage is shaky, our future is cloudy, why not go to the source of all peace? Do we think he will only bless us with wisdom and strength if we are good?

Ask and ye shall find.

They came in too late. They came in for counseling years after the divisions began. By the time they got around to asking for help they had both established different lives. He was involved with another woman. She was alienated and distanced from him. There was no hope left. So they came in and sat there.

"We've decided to get a divorce. It's all very peaceful. We are so happy that this decision has been reached. We just wanted to tell you about it," he explained as he straightened his tie.

She smiled broadly, tucking her right foot behind her left and smoothing down her hair. "It's all very mature," she told me with pride. "We've thought it through and I think we've done an awfully good job of organizing everything."

There was a long silence.

"Okay, then," I finally said. "You don't really need me, do you? "We wanted you to know," he said firmly.

"We thought you would be happy to know how well everything is going!" she beamed again. "I think God would be very proud of how peaceful this divorce is," she paused. I didn't answer. "Right?" she softly said.

What I wanted to say was, "I wish you had come in years ago, when you were a mess and lost and looking much less than perfect. Before all the decisions were made. It's in the mess of it that God can lead us. Not to say that you wouldn't have ended up in the same place as you are right now, but along the way you might have had God's help and strength, and you might have grown spiritually."

But I didn't say it. They had their path. Who am I to say what they should have done? I only know for myself that it is in the mess of my life that I must find the courage to draw near to God. When I do, in those times when I am mature enough to come to God as my true self, I am held by his divine love. And I would not trade that for anything. Not even for looking perfect.

PRAYER:

**Dear God, Deliver me from the need to look perfect. Deliver me into your hands just as I am.
I turn and draw near to you, O Gracious Father.
In Jesus name, Amen.**

47

"**Above all things have intense and unfailing love for one another, for love covers a multitude of sins [forgives and disregards the offenses of others]."**

(1 Peter 4: 8)

Gravy. Love is like gravy. It covers everything with flavor, smooth and silky, transforming meat and potatoes into much more than they might have been otherwise.

All right, that's a little silly. But you get the general idea.

She always looked at him as if he were a movie star. They had been married for a couple of decades. And frankly, he didn't look like much of a movie star. He was a fairly dumpy little guy, his face was slightly smushed, he wore thick glasses, and he was going bald. But the way she watched him, when he would walk over to her, or when he would go to the front of the church and read, you just got the feeling that she thought he was the bee's knees.

She was always saying things to him like, "Gosh, you did that so well," or "I'm so proud of you, Honey." To which he would swell, visibly, stand up a little straighter and kind of give her this shy grin.

They were one of those couples that often held hands. He would open doors for her. She would walk through them with a shy little look at him, always thanking him, always looking kind of amazed that he thought to do such a thing.

I asked her once, "You really seem in love with your husband. Are you? For real?"

"Oh my, yes. Well, who wouldn't be? He is such a charming man. Really, he just ... he just takes my breath away," she flushed as she said this to me.

How must it feel to be the object of such devotion? I think it must feel quite wonderful. It must be like gravy. Like sunlight. Like living in Southern California by the beach. She was so warm to him, without fail, that he actually basked in her love.

Oh, to bask in love.

I didn't see what she saw. But she was looking at him with intense and unfailing love. And this love covered him, and because he was so deeply and intensely loved, the very best part of him was revealed. That is what she saw.

I saw the outside.

She saw the inside.

Sigh.

PRAYER:

Dear God, May I see my spouse with intense and unfailing love. May he/she bask him the gravy of my affection and be covered with the sunlight of agape love. In Jesus name, Amen.

48

"*Give* **thanks in all circumstances, for this is the will of God in Christ Jesus for you."**

(1Thess. 5:18)

Yeah, it is a tricky scripture. Your husband cheats on you and you go and sit in church and hear this scripture, "Give thanks in all circumstances" and your heart is aching so that you can hardly stand up and you just want the world to stop.

It takes a close reading. It does not say, "Give thanks for everything that happens to you."

No. It says, "Give thanks IN all circumstances." *In*. That is the operative word here. *In*.

In the middle of whatever crisis you find yourself in, you can give thanks, because you are not alone. Thank you God for being with me in this dreadful circumstances. What would I do without you? I would fall into the abyss. But here you are, holding me, dragging me back to life., carrying me through this nightmare.

We don't see the bigger picture. We don't know why certain things happen. Someday, of course, I hope that it is all clear. But there is One who does see the big picture. And we can be grateful and thankful and give praise to Him because in all circumstances, he is present with us.

The solid ground is not our marriage, our bank account, our home, or our church. It is God and God alone. Our health may shatter. Our friends may desert us. We may be unjustly persecuted. We may even be crucified. Everything can be shattered except for the reality that we call God.

God is that in which, as the famous phrase puts it, "we live and move and have our being." There is no separation. We can be oblivious of the reality, but God does not shatter.

Two fish are swimming around in the ocean. One says to the other, "Do you believe in water?" The other answers, "Naw, it's just a myth."

Oblivious. And yet, the very reality they are living in.

We are in God.

If we choose to be aware of that, to be awake to that, then we have such a different perspective on the rest of our life.

And that is what we give thanks for; the awareness, the reality, the gift of life itself that can only come from our Creator, Maker and Sustainer.

So don't say, "Thanks for making my life such a mess." That's not true.

Say what is true: "Thanks for being with me, no matter what, in all circumstances."

PRAYER:

Dear God, How often I forget to thank you for simply giving me this life and being with me every step of the way. I thank you now. I thank you for being with me in all the circumstances of my life – the good stuff, the crazy stuff, the wonderful stuff and the hard stuff. I am yours. You are mine. Thanks you. In Jesus name, Amen.

49

"We love because he first loved us. If anyone says, 'I love God,' yet hates his brother, he is a liar. For anyone who does not love his brother, whom he has seen, cannot love God, whom he has not seen. And he has given us this command: Whoever loves God must also love his brother."

(1 John 4)

Whoever loves God must also love his wife. Whoever loves God must also love her husband.

Must, must, must. Could we translate that as, "gets to"?

"Whoever loves God *gets to* also love his wife?"

That is, loving God is not a duty. It is a privilege and so is loving our partners. Rather than seeing worship, study and contemplation of God as a duty, I like to see it as practice. Christian practice. Like football practice. Like dance practice. We get better at it the more we practice.

The same might be applied to marriage.

"What are you doing tonight?" I might ask.

"Oh, I am practicing marriage," you might answer.

And then you'd go home and spend time with your spouse, practicing love. All kinds of love. The friendship kind – talking through the day's events, laughing, having supper, cleaning up after it. The Eros kind – going to bed and making passionate love. The Agape kind – when you lie in each other's arms, after the friendship and the lovemaking and you feel that deeply safe space where you are home.

And you look at each other and say, "Gosh, some really great practice tonight!"

The great artists and athletes never stop practicing. What if we kept at it in marriage – as a privilege?

Get to.

I get to love my husband today.

Wow!

PRAYER:

Dear God, As I practice loving you, may I also extend that privilege to my spouse. May I practice my skills of love with him. May I increase my ability to love day by day. In Jesus name, Amen.

50

"There is no fear in love. But perfect love drives out fear, because fear has to do with punishment. The one who fears is not made perfect in love."

(1 John 4)

The love that this singular and brilliant scrap of scripture is talking about is agape love. It's the big love, the kind that comes from beyond the little minds and hearts of you and me. We do not reach this love or our own. It is given to us, as Christ was given to us. So God gives us a love that does not need to be returned – or understood. And most of all, it does not need to be deserved.

Because agape love is not deserved, we are released from the fear that we will do something to lose it. It cannot be lost.

So much of human behavior is based on survival. Do things right or you will be thrown out of your tribe. In times ancient and modern, being thrown out of the tribe is dangerous. The tribe is safety and food and comfort and protection. So learn what they want you to do and do it.

But God has revealed to us another way, a path that offers a different kind of life. It is not based in survival but it is based in the growth of the soul.

Raising children, we know we must instill in them a healthy fear of electricity, crossing the street, stepping backward off a cliff, not doing homework, eating dirt, acting on every emotion and so on. We must teach them not to jump out the window or hold on to the tail of the cat.

There are things to be afraid of in this world. The problem is that we let this fear bleed over into our spiritual life. In the world of the spirit there are absolutely disciplines, practices, rules and guidelines. And yet, at the very heart of spiritual growth one must release from fear and surrender.

Surrender.

In marriage there are rules, regulations, social expectations, duties, laws, vows and boundaries. At the heart of it, however, in the intimacy of the relationship, is surrender. Without fear I stand before you, just as I am, just as you are, and here, My Beloved, love dwells. Here, I am not afraid.

PRAYER:

Dear God, Teach me to fear that which must be feared. Teach me to surrender to love. In Jesus name, Amen.

51

"God is love. Whoever lives in love lives in God, and God in him. In this way, love is made complete among us so that we will have confidence on the day of judgment, because in this world we are like him."

(1 John 4)

Marriage is a spiritual journey.

On this river I shall set my canoe. It is a canoe with room for two. You have your paddle and I have mine. If we work together we can find the current and ride it.

Here or the current, which is God's power and God's direction, we are carried far beyond our own strength.

You and I.

My bride.

My groom.

The one who knows me through and through.

Who sees me brush my teeth.

Who holds me as I fall asleep.

You and I.

And on this river, when we manage to find the current and steer along staying aloft, we come round the bend and new horizons surprise us.

Knowing the love between us, I have known God.

Living the love between us, I am living in God.

And God in me.

And so it is with gratitude that I thank you for being my partner. It has been a privilege to fall into the river, to right the boat, to bail, to panic, to soar, to spin, to learn and finally to travel with you.

PRAYER:

Dear God, Thank you for giving me the gift of marriage. Thank you. Let me not forget, each day, that it is a blessing. That it is my way to know you. In Jesus name, Amen.

52

"**Love the Lord your God with all your heart and with all your soul and with all your mind and with all your strength. The second is this: 'Love your neighbor as yourself.'"**

(Mark 12:30-31)

And what O Jesus is the greatest commandment? What shall I do with my life, my Master and my Lord?

Love the Lord my God with all my being.

How can I complete such a grand task? How can I begin to hold the ocean that is you in my small and fragile heart?

Ah.

The second commandment, which is like unto the first.

Love your neighbor as yourself.

I look over at my spouse. My neighbor. My closest and nearest neighbor. Close enough to be touched. To be known. To be loved.

Ah.

This I can and will try to do with all my heart.

And all my soul.

And all my mind.

And all my strength.

Thanks for giving me what I can wrap my little human heart around. And through this I shall love you, God?

I shall try.

PRAYER:

Dear God, I love you. In Jesus name, Amen.

ALSO AVAILABLE

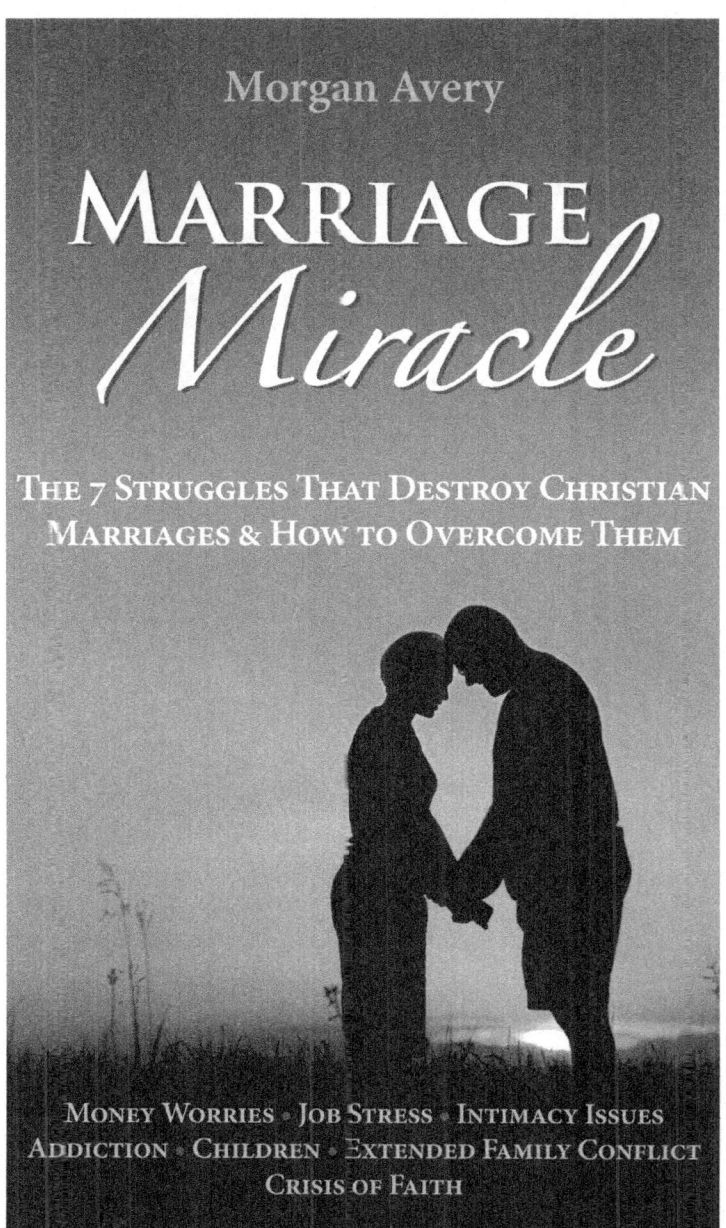

MarriageMiracleOnline.com

CPSIA information can be obtained at www.ICGtesting.com
Printed in the USA
BVOW04s0222100816

458532BV00002B/18/P